My First Book about the Alphabet of Coral Reef Animals
Volume II

Amazing Animal Books
Children's Picture Books

By Molly Davidson

Mendon Cottage Books

JD-Biz Publishing

Read Volume I

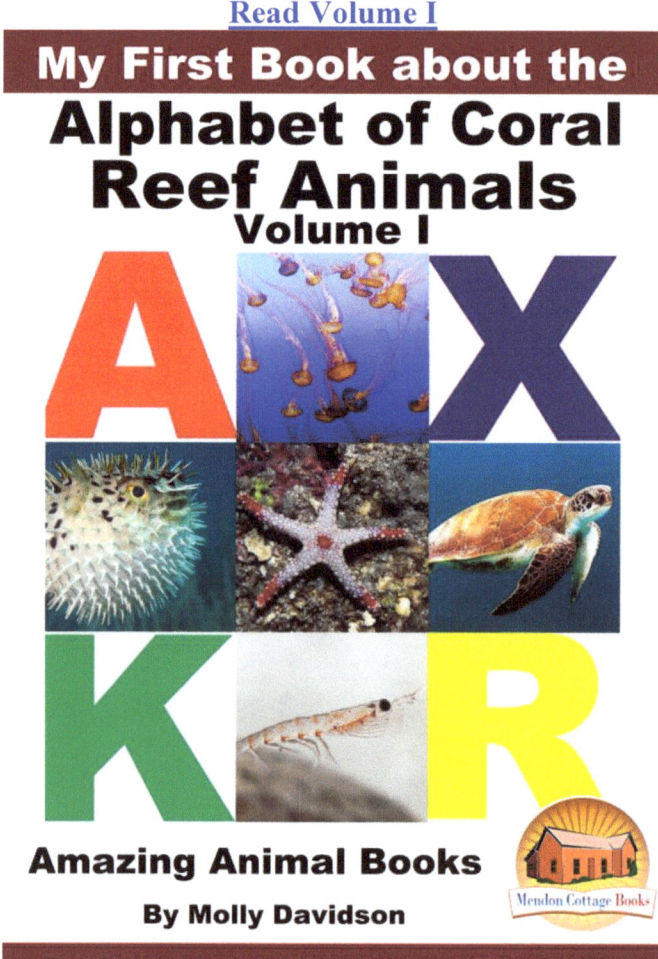

Introduction

Coral reefs are a large group of living organisms, which can grow and shrink.

They create a barrier between the ocean and the coast, acting like protection.

 **is for an Anenome.**

A sea anemone is an animal that stays in one place, and can have between ten and thousands of tentacles.

Their tentacles sting prey as is swims bye, killing it so the anemone can eat.

 **is for a Barracuda.**

Barracudas have long skinny bodies; some grow to be almost 7 feet long.

They have sharp teeth and can swim up to 27 mph, which is how they capture their prey.

C is for a Clownfish.

Clownfish have a protective mucus covering which helps them live in sea anemones without getting stung.

The anemone protects them from predators, and the clownfish keeps the anemone clean by eating its leftovers and algae that starts to grow.

D is for a Diodontidae, the scientific name for a Porcupinefish.

Porcupinefish can gulp down water when in danger to make themselves grow two times bigger and this pokes their sharp spines out.

They swim slowly and usually in large groups.

 is for Echinoderms.

Echinoderms are a species of animal that includes the starfish, sea cucumber, sea urchin, and sand dollar.

They all have five-point radial symmetry, which means they have the exact same five pieces when split from the middle.

F

is for a Foxface Rabbitfish.

Foxface Rabbitfish live in the Indo-Pacific region and are popular in aquariums.

At night and when they are stressed, they will turn a spotted grey color instead of their normal bright yellow.

G is for the Great Hammerhead Shark.

The Great Hammerhead Shark can grow to be up to 20 feet long.

They are an endangered species, due to the fact that they get caught in many fishing nets in coral reefs.

H is for a Houndfish.

Houndfish, also called crocodile needlefish, can grow to be 5 feet long, but weigh only 10 pounds.

They have between 80 - 86 vertebrate in their spine, humans only have 33.

They are known to jump out of the water and puncture fisherman with their sharp beaks.

I is for Isopoda.

Isopoda, also called woodlice, can live in saltwater, freshwater, and on land.

Many feed on the blood of ocean animals, and will attach themselves to their prey.

J is for a Jack.

Jacks are a large fish weighing up to 40 pounds, and growing to 3 feet in length.

They swim by themselves and in groups, called schools, of up to 30.

 **is for Knobby Sea Rod.**

Knobby sea rod is a type of coral found in many of the tropical reefs around the World.

Once they have attached to a solid surface they do not move, but grow larger, usually in big groups, called colonies.

L is for a Leafy Sea Dragon.

Leafy sea dragons are in the same family as sea horses and pipefish.

They live in the Great Barrier Reef, which is along the coast of Australia.

They are wonderful at camouflaging since they look like floating seaweed.

M is for a Moray Eel.

Moray eels are long, like a snake, and have a protective mucus covering.

They hide in caves and rocks found in coral reefs and come out to eat at night.

 is for Nudibranchs.

Nudibranchs are a soft bodied mollusk that doesn't have a shell and are many bright colors.

Many will inject toxins into sponges, so other animals will not eat them, and then the nudibranchs can have it all to themselves.

O is for an Ommastrephidae.

Ommastrephidae are a family of different types of squid, many living in coral reefs.

Their arms and tentacles have sharp teeth which help them catch prey, and then they can bring it to their mouths.

P is for a Pterois, the scientific name for a Lionfish.

Lionfish are a highly venomous fish that lives mostly in the Indo-Pacific area.

They eat many ocean animals and hunt mostly in the morning.

 **is for a Queen Parrotfish.**

Queen parrotfish have many teeth that are sharp and very close together on the outside of their mouths, which forms a sort of beak.

Before they go to sleep they cover themselves in protective mucus this keep predators from smelling them.

R  is for a Reef Stonefish.

Reef stonefish try to blend in with the bottom of the ocean, looking like a rock.

They are known as the most venomous fish in the World, due to their super toxic spines.

S is for a Spotted Trunkfish.

Spotted trunkfish live in the Caribbean coral reefs.

When they are touched they secrete a clear toxin that is only harmful if swallowed, and can kill prey as large as nurse sharks!

T is for a Twospot Cardinalfish.

Belize Larval-Fish Group © Wikimedia Commons

Twospot cardinalfish are a small fish, less than 10 cm long.

They are found in most tropical coral reefs, hiding in dark holes during the day and hunting at night.

To keep their eggs safe the girl will put her eggs inside of the boy's mouth, until they hatch.

U is for Upeneichthys, the scientific name for a Goatfish.

Goatfish have two sharp barbels, like whiskers, on their chin that they use to dig into the sand to find food.

They can change color quickly to blend in with the sand or coral for protection.

 **is for a Variegated Lizardfish.**

Variegated lizardfish can grow to be about 1 1/2 feet long.

They have strong front fins that they use to push off the bottom of the ocean, in order to capture their prey quickly.

W

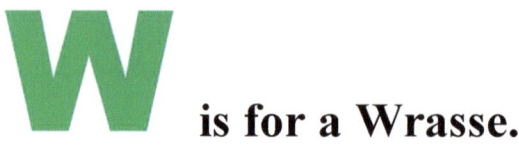

is for a Wrasse.

Wrasses are bright colored tropical reef fish.

They are known as cleaner fish, and help larger predators by eating bacteria and parasites off their back and sometimes in their mouths.

 **X** is for an **Xanthichthys Auromarginatus, the scientific name for a Gilded Triggerfish.**

Gilded triggerfish are usually small, about 8 inches in length and are very friendly.

They can be found in the Indo-Pacific reefs and in many aquariums.

Y

 **is for a Yellow Tang.**

Yellow tang fish can be seen in large numbers around the islands of Hawaii, and are a very popular aquarium fish.

They will clean algae from the shells of sea turtles.

Z is for a Zebra Goby.

Brian Gratwicke © <u>Wikimedia Commons</u>

The zebra goby is a small fish, about 2 inches in length.

They prefer to stay hidden in sea grass, algae, or under rocks.

Conclusion

We hope you have enjoyed the second book on the amazing animals found in coral reefs.

One more fact, coral reefs need lots of sunlight to grow, so this is why most reefs do not exist any deeper than 45 feet below the water.

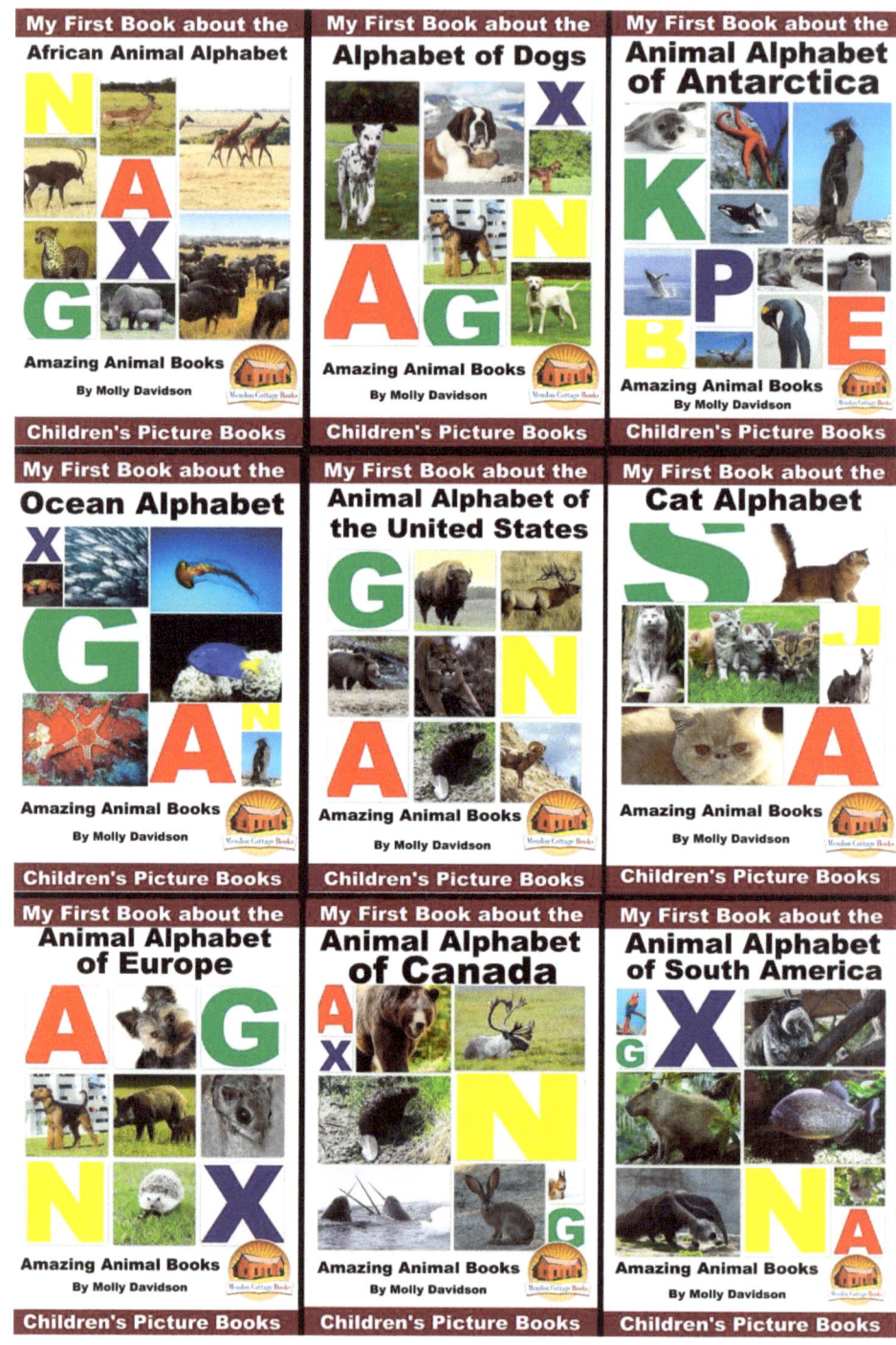

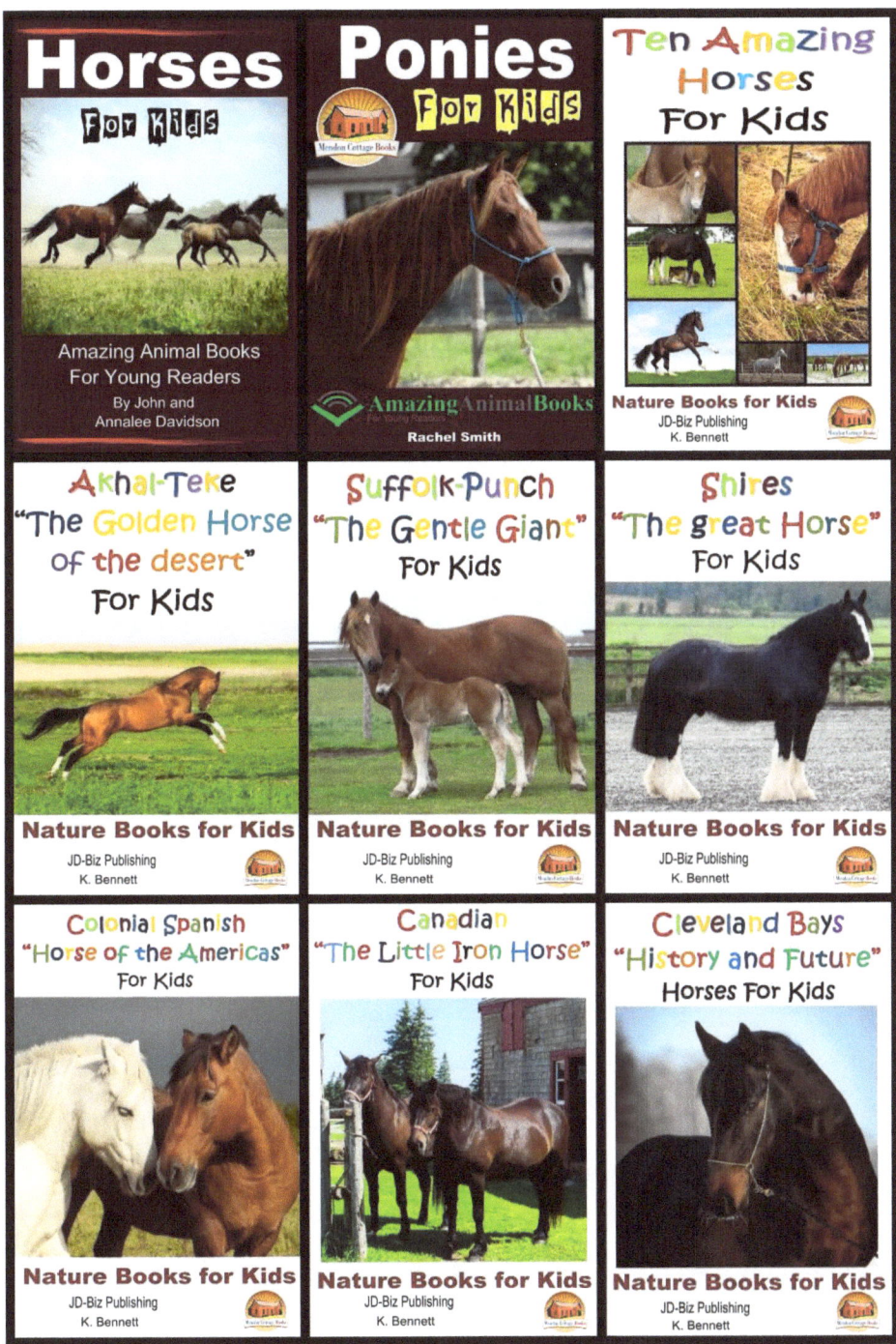

Our books are available at

1. Amazon.com

2. Barnes and Noble

3. Itunes

4. Kobo

5. Smashwords

6. Google Play Books

Download Free Books!
http://MendonCottageBooks.com

Publisher

JD-Biz Corp

P O Box 374

Mendon, Utah 84325

http://www.jd-biz.com/